DISCOVERING THE CARIBBEAN
History, Politics, and Culture

CUBA

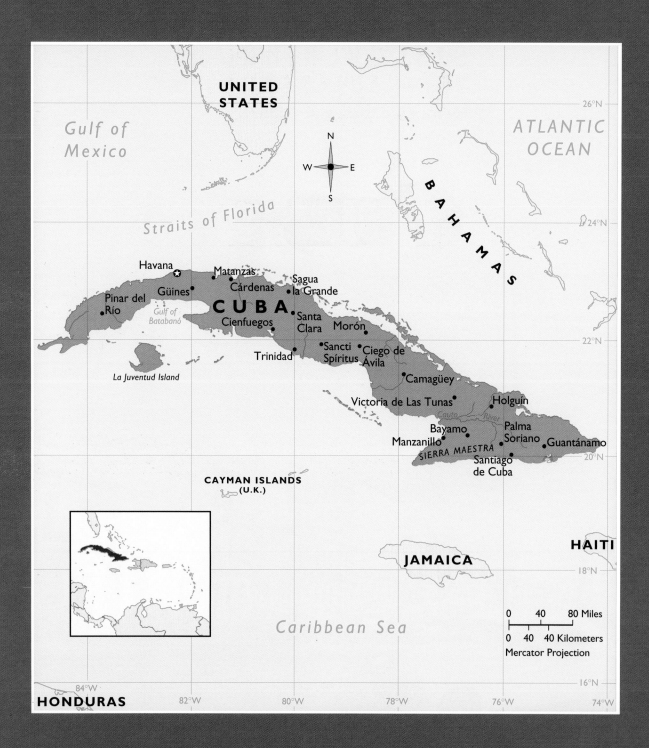

DISCOVERING THE CARIBBEAN
History, Politics, and Culture

CUBA

Roger E. Hernández

Mason Crest
Philadelphia

Mason Crest
450 Parkway Drive, Suite D
Broomall, PA 19008
www.masoncrest.com

Printed and bound in the United States of America.

CPSIA Compliance Information: Batch #DC2015.
For further information, contact Mason Crest at 1-866-MCP-Book.

First printing
1 3 5 7 9 8 6 4 2

Library of Congress Cataloging-in-Publication Data
on file at the Library of Congress

ISBN: 978-1-4222-3310-8 (hc)
ISBN: 978-1-4222-8627-2 (ebook)

Discovering the Caribbean: History, Politics, and Culture series ISBN: 978-1-4222-3307-8

DISCOVERING THE CARIBBEAN: History, Politics, and Culture

Bahamas	Cuba	Leeward Islands
Barbados	Dominican Republic	Puerto Rico
Caribbean Islands:	Haiti	Trinidad & Tobago
Facts & Figures	Jamaica	Windward Islands

TABLE OF CONTENTS

KEY ICONS TO LOOK FOR:

Words to Understand: These words with their easy-to-understand definitions will increase the reader's understanding of the text, while building vocabulary skills.

Sidebars: This boxed material within the main text allows readers to build knowledge, gain insights, explore possibilities, and broaden their perspectives by weaving together additional information to provide realistic and holistic perspectives.

Research Projects: Readers are pointed toward areas of further inquiry connected to each chapter. Suggestions are provided for projects that encourage deeper research and analysis.

Text-Dependent Questions: These questions send the reader back to the text for more careful attention to the evidence presented there.

Series Glossary of Key Terms: This back-of-the book glossary contains terminology used throughout this series. Words found here increase the reader's ability to read and comprehend higher-level books and articles in this field.

Discovering the Caribbean

James D. Henderson

THE CARIBBEAN REGION is a lovely, ethnically diverse part of tropical America. It is at once a sea, rivaling the Mediterranean in size; and it is islands, dozens of them, stretching along the sea's northern and eastern edges. Waters of the Caribbean Sea bathe the eastern shores of Central America's seven nations, as well as those of the South American countries Colombia, Venezuela, and Guyana. The Caribbean islands rise, like a string of pearls, from its warm azure waters. Their sandy beaches, swaying palm trees, and balmy weather give them the aspect of tropical paradises, intoxicating places where time seems to stop.

But it is the people of the Caribbean region who make it a unique place. In their ethnic diversity they reflect their homeland's character as a crossroads of the world for more than five centuries. Africa's imprint is most visible in peoples of the Caribbean, but so too is that of Europe. South and East Asian strains enrich the Caribbean ethnic mosaic as well. Some islanders reveal traces of the region's first inhabitants, the Carib and Taino Indians, who flourished there when Columbus appeared among them in 1492.

Though its sparkling waters and inviting beaches beckon tourists from around the globe, the Caribbean islands provide a significant portion of the world's sugar, bananas, coffee, cacao, and natural fibers. They are strategically important also, for they guard the Panama Canal's eastern approaches.

The Caribbean possesses a cultural diversity rivaling the ethnic kaleido-scope that is its human population. Though its dominant culture is Latin American, defined by languages and customs bequeathed it by Spain and France, significant parts of the Caribbean bear the cultural imprint of

The sun sets over Havana, Cuba.

Northwestern Europe: Denmark, the Netherlands, and most significantly, Britain.

So welcome to the Caribbean! These lavishly illustrated books survey the human and physical geography of the Caribbean, along with its economic and historical development. Geared to the needs of students and teachers, each of the eleven volumes in the series contains a glossary of terms, a chronology, and ideas for class reports. And each volume contains a recipe section featuring tasty, easy-to-prepare dishes popular in the countries dealt with. Each volume is indexed, and contains a bibliography featuring web sources for further information.

Whether old or young, readers of the eleven-volume series DISCOVERING THE CARIBBEAN will come away with a new appreciation of this tropical sea, its jewel-like islands, and its fascinating and friendly people!

Cuba is believed to have been inhabited for nearly 2,000 years, although the original natives of the island were wiped out by Spanish colonization in the 16th century. (Opposite) Tourists enjoy the beach at Varadero. (Right) A farmer in Pinar del Río Province's agricultural Viñales Valley plows his field with oxen.

1 "THE MOST BEAUTIFUL LAND EVER BEHELD"

FOR CENTURIES VISITORS have been enchanted by Cuba's beaches of fine white sand, crystal-clear waters, and luxuriant green countryside, graced by majestic palms that sway in the tropical breeze. "The most beautiful land ever beheld by human eyes," Christopher Columbus is said to have exclaimed when he first arrived in Cuba.

When most people think of the modern-day nation of Cuba, they picture a single island—the one Columbus so enthusiastically described in late October of 1492. In reality, the Republic of Cuba is made up of as many as 4,000 *cays* and islets surrounding the biggest island in the *archipelago*, which is also called Cuba. That island of Cuba is the largest in the Greater Antilles, and the largest in the entire Caribbean Sea. Cuba is located between the North Atlantic Ocean and the Caribbean Sea, at the entrance of the Gulf of

Mexico. It is only 90 miles (145 kilometers) from the tip of Florida, the southernmost point of the continental United States.

The long, slender main island takes up 40,519 square miles (104,904 sq km), all but about 2,000 square miles (5,178 sq km) of the nation's total area. It is 782 miles (1,258 km) in length from east to west, but only 120 miles (193 km) at its widest point and a mere 20 miles (32 km) at its narrowest. The largest of the outlying islands is Isla de Pinos, or Isla de la Juventud. With an area of 849 square miles (2,198 sq km), it is the only other Cuban island that has traditionally been populated.

The rest of the cays are divided into four chains. Los Colorados and Sabana-Camagüey are off the northern coast of the main island, with Los Canarreos and Jardines de la Reina in the south. Most are undeveloped and uninhabited. Two exceptions are Cayo Coco and Cayo Largo, which boast new tourist resorts.

About two-thirds of the main island was originally covered by flat wooded meadows or tropical grasslands called savannas. Much of it is now used for farming or was cleared to build villages and towns. These plains are interrupted by mountains. The Sierra de los Organos and Sierra del Rosario are in

Words to Understand in This Chapter

archipelago—a group of neighboring islands.
cay—a small sandy island or coral reef.
endemic—native to a particular area and existing nowhere else.

the west. In the center lies the Sierra del Escambray. The extreme east has several chains, including the Sierra de Moa, Sierra de Nipe, Sierra de Cristal, and Sierra Maestra, the highest of all. *Mogotes*, a formation unique to the western end of the island, are rounded mounds covered in vegetation that abruptly rise, to a height of several stories, from otherwise perfectly flat valley floors.

The main island's 2,320 miles (3,734 km) of coastline are extremely diverse. There are picturesque beaches, well-protected natural bays, sheer cliffs, marshes, and even near-desert. Cuba's largest swamp is the Ciénaga de Zapata, located on a shoe-shaped peninsula along the south coast.

The trogon is considered the national bird of Cuba, as its colors remind Cubans of their flag.

The country's rivers are numerous, but short and shallow. The largest is the Cauto, 230 miles (370 km) long, of which less than a third is navigable. There are no large lakes. Overall, Cuba has only 150 miles (241 km) of waterway.

On the southeast coast of Cuba lies Guantánamo Bay, a sheltered natural channel. Since shortly after the Spanish-American War in 1898, the United States has maintained a naval base there, despite poor relations with Cuba.

Climate

Cool trade winds moderate Cuba's tropical climate even in the hottest months. The average summer temperature is 77°F (25°C); average winter temperatures are cooler by a mere 5°F (3°C). The dry season runs from November

Panoramic view of Sierra del Escambray mountains in central Cuba.

to April; the wet season, from May to October. The last three months of the rainy season are often wetter than Cubans would like—this is hurricane season. Tropical storms hit Cuba most years, sometimes causing loss of life and widespread property damage. In 2012, Hurricane Sandy hit the province of Santiago, killing 11 people and damaging more than 100,000 homes.

ANIMALS AND PLANTS

Cuba has a tremendous variety of exotic flowers and tropical shrubs. Trees include the stately royal palm, the fiery red *flamboyán*, the wide-branched algarroba, and the ceiba, which can reach 150 feet (46 meters) in diameter and 100 feet (31 meters) in height. Mangroves grow in areas of shallow salt water, their tall, gnarled root systems often exposed at low tide. More than half of Cuba's vegetation is *endemic*.

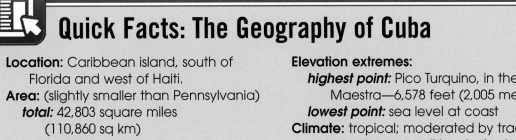

Quick Facts: The Geography of Cuba

Location: Caribbean island, south of Florida and west of Haiti.
Area: (slightly smaller than Pennsylvania)
 total: 42,803 square miles (110,860 sq km)
 land: 42,803 square miles (110,860 sq km)
 water: 0 square miles
Borders: U.S. naval base at Guantánamo Bay, 18 miles (29 km).
Terrain: mostly flat savannas and rolling hills, with mountains in southeast.

Elevation extremes:
 highest point: Pico Turquino, in the Sierra Maestra—6,578 feet (2,005 meters).
 lowest point: sea level at coast
Climate: tropical; moderated by trade winds; dry season (Nov. to Apr.); rainy season (May to Oct.).
Natural hazards: hurricanes, which may hit from August to October, droughts.

Source: CIA World Factbook 2015.

Cuba also boasts rich animal life, with 900 fish, 4,000 mollusk (shellfish), 146 reptile, and 350 bird species. Among the birds are hawks, flamingos, parrots, ducks, songbirds, the bee hummingbird (at 2.5 inches, or 6.4 centimeters, the smallest bird in the world), and the Cuban trogon. Among the reptiles are snakes, more than 90 species of lizards and iguanas, giant sea turtles, and two species of crocodiles. There aren't many mammals, though. Of the 38 native species, 27 are bats and 10 are *jutías*, large wild rodents. The other species, which looks like a rat, is the rare, insect-eating Cuban *solenodon*. Deer and wild boar are also present but are not native to the island.

TEXT-DEPENDENT QUESTIONS

1. What is Cuba's largest river?
2. Why is the trogon considered the national bird of Cuba?

Since the arrival of the Spanish in the late 15th century, Cuba has been a land in turmoil. (Opposite) Statue of José Martí, who worked for Cuban independence during the 19th century, in Cienfuegos. (Right) This mural of revolutionary leader Ernesto "Che" Guevara appears on a wall of the Ministerio del Interior in Havana.

2 FROM CONQUISTADORS TO CASTROS

CUBA'S ORIGINAL INHABITANTS were Arawak Indian tribes. The Guanahatabeyes, who occupied the western part of the island, were the most primitive. They lived in caves and hewed rough tools of stone and seashell. The Siboneyes lived in the center. They made refined ceremonial objects of stone and wood. The most advanced of Cuba's Indians were the Tainos, who lived in the center and east. They dwelled in towns of thatched-roof houses called *bohíos*, farmed, and made pottery.

Although most of the Arawak were wiped out after the Spanish arrived, they left a legacy: Cuban Indians introduced tobacco to the conquistadors, and from them it spread to the rest of the world. Beyond that, nothing of their culture remains except for the *bohíos* still seen in the countryside and Taino words like "hurricane," "hammock," and "tobacco."

CONQUEST AND COLONIZATION

Christopher Columbus landed in Cuba on October 27, 1492, during his first trip to the New World. However, the Spanish made no attempt to colonize the island until two decades later, when an expedition led by Diego Velázquez was sent to Cuba. Velázquez established several communities, including Baracoa, Santiago, and Havana. Today, these are among Cuba's largest and most important cities.

Words to Understand in This Chapter

Cold War—a political and economic conflict between the United States and the Soviet Union, which lasted from 1945 until 1991 and which included regional wars between allies of the two nations but no direct fighting between them.

Communist—characteristic of communism, an economic system under which goods and services are produced by the government, with no private enterprise permitted; or, a person who supports communism.

dissidents—those who disagree with a political system, particularly in a dictatorship.

embargo—a ban on trade with a particular country or countries.

exile—a period of absence from one's native country, often to escape repressive conditions; also, a person who has left his or her country under those circumstances.

galleon—a large ship with square sails that was used especially by the Spanish during the colonial period to transport treasure from the Americas to Spain.

guerrillas—armed fighters who are not part of a regular army and who typically use hit-and-run tactics.

nationalize—to remove control and ownership of a business from private hands and transfer it to the government.

The first Spaniards in Cuba were primarily seeking gold, but they also established farms and plantations. Labor was not a problem: the colonists forced Indians to work the mines and till the fields. Within 30 years, nearly the entire native population had died as the result of exhaustion, disease, or fighting with the Spaniards. To replace them, the colonists brought enslaved blacks from Africa.

By the 1600s it was apparent that Cuba held little gold. But many colonists started plantations of tobacco and sugarcane, which became Cuba's most important product. Cuba also became a major trading post. Spanish *galleons* laden with gold and silver from the mines of Mexico and Peru met in Havana's harbor before crossing the Atlantic Ocean to Spain. To fight off pirates, the treasure ships were guarded by warships.

The Spanish colonies in Cuba grew and prospered. In 1774, according to a census, Havana had a population of 75,618, making it larger than any North American city. But many Cubans did not share in the island's prosperity. Under Spanish law colonies were permitted to trade only with Spain, not with other colonies or countries. This ensured that the trade would most benefit people in Spain, who could control the prices of imports from, and exports to, the colonies.

The cumbersome and one-sided system lasted until 1762, when Great Britain occupied Havana. The British stayed for just one year before giving the city back to Spain. But they left their mark. Under their rule, Cubans were allowed to trade freely. Many became wealthy, and for the first time they started to see themselves as Cubans instead of Spaniards who happened to be born in Cuba.

WARS OF INDEPENDENCE

Beginning around 1810, wars of independence flared throughout the Spanish colonies in Mexico, Central America, and South America. By the mid-1820s most of Spain's once vast empire in the Americas had broken away. Cuba, however, didn't rebel against Spanish rule. By the 1840s Cuba and Puerto Rico were Spain's last remaining outposts in the Western Hemisphere.

Remaining a Spanish colony had major drawbacks for the Cuban *criollos*—whites of pure Spanish extraction who had been born in Cuba. Though they were the society's wealthiest and best-educated members, the criollos couldn't aspire to the top positions in government. Those positions were reserved for *peninsulares*—Spaniards born in Spain—who often seemed to look down on those they governed. Cubans who complained about the situation might find themselves in prison. Still, white Cubans were reluctant to rebel—largely because many feared that slaves would take over the island if the Spanish left.

Some Cubans *did* want to rule themselves, however. In the 1820s a Catholic priest named Félix Varela worked to make Cuba independent. When Spanish authorities tried to put him in jail, he escaped to New York. He was among the first of many Cubans who have gone into **exile** in the United States to escape oppressive governments. Several other attempts to gain independence failed.

In 1868 Carlos Manuel de Céspedes, a rich planter, freed his slaves and took up arms against the Spanish. This marked the start of the Ten Years War. More than 250,000 people, including Céspedes, died in the conflict. Sugar mills were left in ruins. After a decade of fighting, Spain finally put down the rebellion. The Spanish government promised Cubans freedom and equality. Although slaves on the island were freed, Spain did not deliver on most of its promises.

Cubans continued to plot for independence. Thousands became exiles in the United States. One of them was José Martí, who arrived in New York in 1880. Martí wrote some of the greatest poems in the Spanish language, and he was also renowned for his skill as a writer of political essays. But he is just as well known for leading the struggle to end Spanish rule. Traveling between Cuban exile communities in New York and Florida, he raised money and convinced veterans of the Ten Years War to join his cause. In 1895, he returned to Cuba and launched the War of Independence. Unfortunately, Martí was killed in battle barely a month after the war started.

Cuban leaders like Máximo Gómez, Calixto García, and Antonio Maceo (the highest-ranking black officer) continued the war. Along with Martí, all are legendary figures in Cuban history.

As fighting dragged on through 1898, the United States sent the battleship *Maine* to Cuba to protect American property and citizens. But the ship exploded while anchored in Havana Harbor. Although the cause has never been determined, the United States

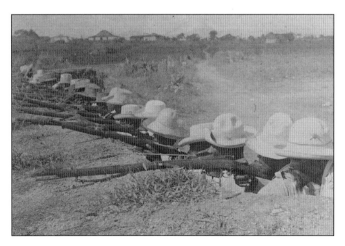

Cuban soldiers await a Spanish attack in a trench near Pinar del Rio, 1899.

blamed Spain for the explosion and declared war. Americans and Cubans, fighting together, defeated Spanish forces in a few months.

For the next four years Cuba was ruled by the United States. Finally, on May 20, 1902, Cuba became independent.

THE REPUBLICAN ERA

Some Cubans complained that their country was not fully independent, however. The Platt Amendment to the Cuban Constitution gave the United States the right to intervene in Cuban affairs. And the Americans *did* intervene. When rivals tried to overthrow President Tomás Estrada Palma, the United States sent troops to stop the fighting. The United States ruled Cuba again from 1906 to 1909. A period of calm followed, with a free press and elections. But many of Cuba's leaders were corrupt.

In 1924 Gerardo Machado was elected president. When his term was over, he refused to leave. He killed political opponents and censored the press. Machado ruled as Cuba's first dictator until he was toppled in 1933.

After the fall of the Machado government, U.S. president Franklin D. Roosevelt abolished the Platt Amendment, making Cuba truly independent. But trouble still dogged the island. Political factions fought in the streets. There were eight changes of government in the three years after Machado's fall.

Through it all, a leader in the Cuban military named Fulgencio Batista controlled politics behind the scenes. In 1940 Batista was elected president under a new constitution. After a four-year term, he stepped aside for newly elected president Ramón Grau San Martín. Four years later, a new president, Carlos Prío Socarrás, took office.

During the eight years that Grau and Prío governed, Cubans had never been so free and prosperous. Unfortunately, the two leaders allowed their subordinates to get away with massive corruption. When the dishonesty came to light, the Ortodoxo Party was created, and the country waited for the election of 1952.

The election was never held. With the support of the military, Batista chased Prío out of the country and made himself dictator.

Many Cubans did not like Batista. Among them was a young lawyer named Fidel Castro. In 1953, Castro organized an attack on the Moncada army barracks in Santiago. The rebels were defeated and Castro was captured and jailed.

Castro was released from jail less than two years later. In Mexico, he and Argentinean revolutionary Ernesto "Che" Guevara organized the 26th of July Movement (named for the date of the Moncada attack) to fight Batista. In 1956 they landed in Oriente Province with 80 armed men. Batista's troops hunted the revolutionaries down in the Sierra Maestra, killing all but a handful. But opposition to Batista grew. Peasants joined Castro's men to launch *guerrilla* attacks on army posts. They placed bombs in the cities and harassed Batista's police. Workers, business leaders, professionals, and intellectuals supported Castro. Eventually Batista's own soldiers did not want to fight.

Fulgencio Batista ruled Cuba for most of the 1940s and 1950s.

On January 1, 1959, Batista fled and Fidel Castro became the new leader of Cuba.

THE CASTRO ERA

Castro came to power with overwhelming popular support. Many Cubans thought democracy had finally arrived on their island. But the new government began to jail and execute opponents, censor the press, and *nationalize* private property. Many Cubans who had at first supported Castro turned against him, saying he was trying to set up a *Communist* dictatorship.

When the U.S. government broke off diplomatic relations, Castro asked for the support of the Soviet Union, the main rival of the United States during the *Cold War*. Many Castro opponents fled to Miami, Florida.

In April of 1961, a United States–backed army of Cuban exiles known as Brigade 2506 landed on the southern coast of Cuba at the Bay of Pigs. They were quickly defeated by Castro's troops. Late that year Castro publicly declared Cuba a Communist country, outlawing other political parties. The United States imposed an *embargo*, prohibiting American companies and individuals from trading with Cuba. In response, Cuba became even closer to the Soviet Union.

Another crisis took place in October 1962, when President John F. Kennedy announced there were Soviet nuclear missiles in Cuba and demanded they be removed. For a few days, the world teetered on the brink of nuclear war. Then the Soviets withdrew their missiles, on the condition that the United States remove missiles from Turkey and prevent Cuban exiles from organizing another invasion of the island.

Through the 1960s the Castro government continued to jail and execute political opponents. But it also improved literacy, housing, and health care. Today the regime points to the success of those efforts as a triumph of the Cuban Revolution. Opponents reply that Cuba was among the most advanced nations in the Latin America even before Castro, and note that progress did not have to mean the end of political freedom in Cuba.

Beginning in the 1960s, the Castro government also began providing support to Communist guerrillas in Latin American countries like Venezuela, Colombia, Bolivia, and Nicaragua, as well as in African countries like Angola and Ethiopia.

People continued trying to escape Castro's Cuba, but to leave the country legally they needed government permission. In April 1980, after a number of his opponents took refuge in the Peruvian embassy in Havana, Castro announced that anyone who wished could leave freely from the port of Mariel. Tens of thousands of Cubans departed their country in rickety boats, heading for Florida. More than 125,000 people had fled the island by the time the government reimposed restrictions.

The Castro government's policy of not permitting political opposition

After forcing Batista out in 1959, Fidel Castro took over Cuba's government. He stayed in power until 2008.

drew criticism from organizations such as Human Rights Watch and Amnesty International. Groups of *dissidents* demanding more freedom sprang up, but they were often jailed, harassed by pro-government mobs, and denied employment.

But the early 1990s also brought a huge blow to Castro's Cuba. For years the Cuban economy had been propped up with heavy financial support from the Soviet Union. Following the collapse of the Soviet Union and the end of communism in much of the world, Cuba found itself without the support of its primary trading partner. Shortages of food, oil, electricity, clothing, and just about everything else became more acute than ever. With little money, Castro was forced to stop directly aiding revolutionary movements overseas.

After a string of lean years, the Cuban economy rebounded somewhat in the late 1990s, led by tourism from Canada, Europe, and Latin America. However, U.S. embargo laws continued to prevent Americans from visiting Cuba, depriving Castro's government of a potentially vast source of tourist revenue. A 1998 visit to Cuba by Pope John Paul II, and a 2002 trip by former U.S. president Jimmy Carter, raised hopes for reform within Cuba and for better U.S.-Cuba relations.

Thawing Relations

In 2008, Fidel Castro retired as president of Cuba at the age of 81. His brother Raúl, who is four years younger, replaced him. Many people thought that nothing would change, but Raúl Castro soon began implementing reforms to Cuban society. He lifted some restrictions on goods that consumers were allowed to purchase, from cars to computers, and also began to make economic changes, such as allowing small privately owned businesses to operate, and letting farmers sell their produce directly to consumers, rather than through state-owned stores. His government also took steps to encourage foreign investment in tourist resorts and hotels. In 2011, Raúl Castro relaxed additional government regulations in hopes of stimulating economic growth. The government also granted amnesty to thousands of political prisoners.

Since becoming president of Cuba in 2008, Raúl Castro has implemented many reforms.

Most Cubans supported these changes, and in February 2013 the National Assembly reelected Raúl Castro to a second five-year term as president. The international community welcomed the changes as well. In December 2014, U.S. President Barack Obama announced that the two countries were in talks to end the U.S. embargo and normalize relations. In early 2015, some American travel and trade restrictions on Cuba were eased, and in April President Obama announced that Cuba would be removed from a list of countries that the United States believes sponsor international terrorism.

TEXT-DEPENDENT QUESTIONS

1. What Cuban poet encouraged a revolution against the Spanish in 1895?

2. What was the name of the movement organized by Fidel Castro and Ernesto "Che" Guevara? Why was the movement given this name?

Under Castro, Cuba became one of the poorest countries in the Caribbean. (Opposite) Shoppers sample the wares in a street market in Havana. (Right) Cubans work in the Partagas cigar factory in Havana, established in 1845. The workers earn less per day than the cost of one cigar in Europe or Japan.

3 A STRUGGLING ECONOMY

CUBA'S ECONOMY IS different from that of *capitalist* nations like the United States, because it is based on Communist principles. These principles are that all citizens should share work equally and share wealth equally. To accomplish this, communism advocates the elimination of private property. So in Cuba, the government—not individuals or corporations—owns most of the factories and farmland and controls most commerce.

Since this system was put in place in the early 1960s, the Cuban economy has declined. In the mid-1950s, Cuba ranked third among 19 Latin American and Caribbean nations in gross domestic product (GDP) per capita, a measure of each person's share in the economic value of goods and services produced in a year. In 2014, Cuba was ranked 23rd of 33 nations by this measure. Each Cuban family is only allowed to buy a certain amount of goods—even basic items such as food, clothing, and consumer products.

Some blame the problems on the Communist economy. Others blame the embargo imposed by the United States. Whatever the case, things got worse in the early 1990s after the Soviet Union stopped providing Cuba with an estimated $4 billion to $6 billion in *subsidies* each year.

With Cuba facing an economic crisis, in recent years the Raúl Castro government has implemented free-market reforms, such as allowing foreign companies to invest in tourist resorts and permitting self-employment—with restrictions—in some 150 occupations. Recent moves include permitting the private ownership and sale of real estate and new vehicles, allowing private farmers to sell agricultural goods directly to hotels, and expanding categories of self-employment. As a result, the economy has improved in recent years. However, despite these reforms the average Cuban's standard of living remains at a lower level than before the collapse of the Soviet Union and the economic downturn of the 1990s.

Words to Understand in This Chapter

arable—suitable for growing crops.
biotechnology—the use of biological knowledge to make products such as medicines.
black market—the selling or buying of goods in violation of official regulations, or a place where goods are sold illegally.
capitalist—supporting capitalism, an economic system under which goods and services are produced by private enterprise, with little participation from the government.
subsidies—grants or gifts of money to help sustain a non-profitable venture.

Agriculture

Agricultural products are Cuba's leading export, and about one-fifth of the country's workforce is involved in agriculture. The main crop has for centuries been sugarcane, which covers nearly three-quarters of Cuba's *arable* land.

A tobacco farmer cuts leaves in the Viñales Valley, Pinar del Río, Cuba. Tobacco is one of Cuba's most important crops.

Tobacco is the island's second most important export crop. Cuba has the second-largest area planted with tobacco of all countries in the world. The island is particularly known for its cigars, with those produced in the western region of Vuelta Abajo said to be the world's best.

Economic reforms passed in 2011 allowed individual farmers to sell fruits and vegetables directly to consumers, rather than to state agencies for resale through their stores. This has helped to reduce waste and eliminate black-market sales.

For all its fertile land, Cuba is not agriculturally self-sufficient. Each year the government must import several billion dollars worth of foodstuffs, along with all farm machinery, and most pesticides, fertilizers, and fuel for farm equipment. Almost one-sixth of the total amount of food that Cubans consume annually is imported from other countries.

INDUSTRY

Industry employs about one-sixth of the Cuban workforce. Most of Cuba's industry is based on the refining of agricultural products. Not only is sugarcane Cuba's leading crop, but it also provides the raw material for the country's leading industrial product, sugar. There are approximately 150 sugar mills on the island. Sugarcane is also used to make rum, a long-standing Cuban export. Another major agricultural product requiring processing is tobacco. Much of the work continues to be done manually by craftsmen who roll cigars in the traditional, centuries-old way.

Other industry is of lesser importance. Cuba has some cement and steel

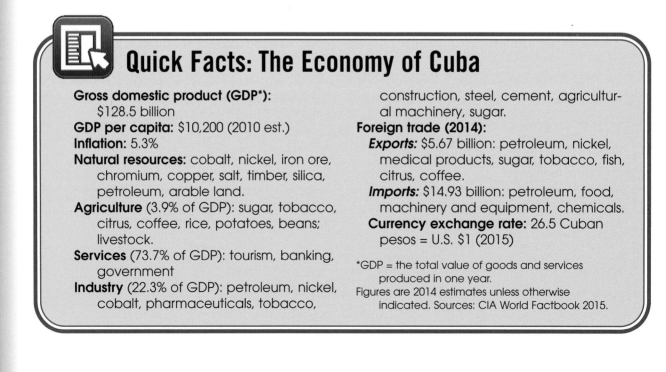

Quick Facts: The Economy of Cuba

Gross domestic product (GDP*): $128.5 billion

GDP per capita: $10,200 (2010 est.)

Inflation: 5.3%

Natural resources: cobalt, nickel, iron ore, chromium, copper, salt, timber, silica, petroleum, arable land.

Agriculture (3.9% of GDP): sugar, tobacco, citrus, coffee, rice, potatoes, beans; livestock.

Services (73.7% of GDP): tourism, banking, government

Industry (22.3% of GDP): petroleum, nickel, cobalt, pharmaceuticals, tobacco, construction, steel, cement, agricultural machinery, sugar.

Foreign trade (2014):

    Exports: $5.67 billion: petroleum, nickel, medical products, sugar, tobacco, fish, citrus, coffee.

    Imports: $14.93 billion: petroleum, food, machinery and equipment, chemicals.

    Currency exchange rate: 26.5 Cuban pesos = U.S. $1 (2015)

*GDP = the total value of goods and services produced in one year.
Figures are 2014 estimates unless otherwise indicated. Sources: CIA World Factbook 2015.

manufacturing as well as oil refineries. The government has invested in *biotechnology*, and exports medicinal products to Venezuela and other countries. In recent years, the government has tried to encourage foreign investment in order to modernize Cuba's aging industrial plants. It allows joint ventures in which foreign companies put up the money, but the Cuban government maintains partial ownership of the factories.

Mining

Cuba's most important export product after sugar is nickel. Cuba is the sixth-largest producer of nickel in the world. Its principal mines are in the eastern provinces, where the mineral deposits are located close to the surface and are relatively cheap to extract. Processing takes place in three plants, which are being modernized with Canadian and European investment. The government also hopes to increase production of cobalt; Cuba is the world's tenth-largest producer of this metallic element.

There is also some foreign exploration for oil and natural gas, mostly by Russian and Venezuelan oil companies . However, proven reserves in Cuba are small: about 300 million barrels of oil and 300 to 600 trillion cubic feet of natural gas. This provides only about 10 percent of Cuba's needs, nowhere near enough to end Cuba's dependence on foreign fuel. Some $700 million worth of gas and oil must be imported annually. Most of this comes from Venezuela, a country that Cuba has had a close relationship with since the early 2000s. Cuba has been paying for the oil, in part, with the services of Cuban personnel in Venezuela, including some 30,000 medical professionals.

A tourist takes photos in the town of Trinidad. Tourism is the strongest sector of Cuba's economy. Most visitors come from Canada, then Europe. Although travel to Cuba was restricted for U.S. citizens, typically between 30,000 and 60,000 Americans visited Cuba each year despite the embargo.

SERVICES

Government is the largest employer—not surprising in an economy in which the state owns all media and financial offices, save for a few foreign banks. More than 60 percent of all Cuban workers hold service-sector jobs.

Tourism is the fastest-growing part of the economy. In the mid-1990s it surpassed sugar as Cuba's largest source of foreign exchange. The government advertises heavily to attract visitors from Europe, Latin America, and Canada. More than 3 million foreigners visit Cuba each year. Yet tourism has become a source of friction, because resorts are off-limits to ordinary Cubans.

Foreign investment in tourism resulted in a marked increase in the number of hotel rooms, from 12,000 in 1990 to 35,000 just 10 years later. As in manufacturing, companies that invest in Cuban resorts must give 50 percent of ownership to the state.

In recent years, more than 200,000 Cubans have become *cuentapropistas*, or entrepreneurs. Many of them work in tourism-related jobs such as driving cabs, guiding visitor groups, or serving dinners at *paladares*, restaurants that the government allows to operate in licensed private homes.

Cuba also has a **black market**, in which Cubans with U.S. dollars (often sent by friends or relatives in the United States) can buy food staples and household goods not available in the legal economy. In 2015, President Obama increased the amount of money that Americans could legally send to Cuba from $2,000 a year to $8,000 a year, and experts predicted that increased remittances would help to stimulate the Cuban economy.

TEXT-DEPENDENT QUESTIONS

1. Where does Cuba rank in GDP per capita?
2. How many sugar mills are located on Cuba?
3. What country provides much of the oil that Cuba imports?

Cuba is known throughout the world for its vibrant culture, which blends Spanish and African influences. (Opposite) a group of young Cubans in costume during a Carnival celebration in Santiago de Cuba. (Right) An altar for Cuba's Santeria religion, which combines elements of Roman Catholicism and African spirit worship.

4 Joy in Life: Cuba's Culture and People

ABOUT ONE QUARTER of all Cubans are of mixed heritage—that is, they claim mixed black and white (mulatto) or mixed white and Amerindian (mestizo) ancestry. Almost all of the rest are either white or black. Unlike other Latin American nations, Cuba has a very small Indian population. A small minority (about 1 percent) of Cubans are ethnic Chinese, the descendants of laborers who arrived from China in the mid-1800s. At one point, Cuba was also home to a sizable Jewish population as the result of immigration from eastern Europe and Turkey. But after Castro came to power, most Jews left.

Cuba's culture, a rich blend of Spanish and African influences, began to take shape in the late 18th and early 19th centuries. At that time residents of Spanish extraction started to view themselves as Cuban rather than Spanish, and blacks whose ancestors were slaves from Africa became "Cubanized" too.

EVERYDAY LIFE

Cubans have the reputation throughout the Spanish-speaking world of being a joyful, life-loving people, hospitable and hardworking. For Cubans, as for other Latins, family is extremely important. Grandparents traditionally live near their adult children, if not in the same house. It is also customary for children to live with their parents until marriage.

On a typical day, Cubans have a light breakfast, a big meal in the afternoon called the *almuerzo*, and dinner in the evening. Rice is a part of every meal except breakfast. It is accompanied by beans, **tubers** such as yucca and *malanga*, and, when available, chicken, pork, or beef. The most traditional dish is white rice and black beans, which reflects the nation's white Spanish and black African legacy not just in the way it looks, but also in its traditional name: Moors and Christians.

This dual Spanish-African heritage influenced religion too. Before the Cuban Revolution, most Cubans were Catholic, but a significant number practiced **Santeria**, a mix of Catholic and African tribal beliefs. The Revolution, however, discourages religion. Christmas festivities were sus-

Words to Understand in This Chapter

tubers—foods that are part of a plant's underground root system, such as potatoes.
Santeria—a religious system that developed in Cuba, and blends beliefs and customs of the Yoruba people of West Africa with elements of the Roman Catholic religion.

Quick Facts: The People of Cuba

Population: 11,047,251
Ethnic groups: white 64.1%, mestizo 26.6%, black 9.3% (2012).
Age structure:
0–14 years: 16.3%
15–64 years: 71.1%
65 years and over: 12.6%
Population growth rate: -0.14%
Birth rate: 9.9 births/1,000 population.
Death rate: 7.64 deaths/1,000 population.
Infant mortality rate: 4.7 deaths/1,000 live births.
Life expectancy at birth: 78.22 years.

male: 75.92 years.
female: 80.65 years.
Total fertility rate: 1.46 children born per woman.
Religions: nominally Roman Catholic 85%, Protestant, Jehovah's Witnesses, Jewish, Santeria.
Languages: Spanish (official).
Literacy rate (age 15 and older who can read and write): 99.8% (2012).

All figures are 2014 estimates unless otherwise noted.
Source: CIA World Factbook 2015.

pended in the 1960s and not permitted again until 1998, following the visit of Pope John Paul II. In April 2012, Cuba observed Good Friday (the Friday before Easter Sunday) with a public holiday for the first time since the gained control of the island in 1959.

Sports play a big role in Cuban life. The nation has long produced major-league-caliber baseball players and Olympic champion boxers. Under Castro, all sports are amateur, although the top athletes receive strong support from the government. Cubans do very well in the Olympics, and the national baseball team is among the best in the world.

The Cuban government does not allow players to go to the United States to play baseball. However, a growing number of players have managed to make it to the major leagues in recent years. They include pitcher Aroldis

Young Cubans play baseball on a field along the Malecon in Havana.

Chapman, slugging first baseman José Abreu, and outfielders Yoenis Céspedes and Yasiel Puig. In 2014, the Boston Red Sox signed Rusney Castillo to a seven-year contract worth $72.5 million—the largest contract ever given to a Cuban defector.

Cuban children must attend school until ninth grade. There are more than 12,000 elementary and high schools on the island, along with six universities. But professionals do not have an opportunity to earn much under

Cuba's Communist system. Doctors, engineers, and scientists often work as waiters or taxi drivers in order to earn dollars in tips from tourists.

Economic shortages affect the everyday life of most Cubans. They must spend time finding stores where the goods they seek are available, and then they must wait in long lines with ration books in hand. However, Cubans don't need to worry about health care or retirement. Cuba's social security program guarantees money in case of disability or retirement. In addition, health care in Cuba is free, and the ratio of doctors and hospitals to citizens is among the best in Latin America. Doctors are available in rural as well as urban areas. However, the deterioration of the Cuban economy after the loss of Soviet aid, as well as the continuing American embargo, have led to chronic shortages of medicine and medical supplies.

The Castro regime has long blamed the American embargo for all of Cuba's economic woes. Yet for many ordinary Cubans, American popular culture holds significant appeal. Cubans love American movies. They also have a large appetite for American food, blue jeans, and consumer products, though these items are in short supply. And the streets of Havana are full of classic American cars from the 1950s, many maintained with homemade spare parts. Since the U.S. embargo began, Cuba has had difficulty importing automobiles, and until recently, Cubans were only allowed to buy or sell vehicles that had been on the road before the 1959 revolution.

THE ARTS AND MUSIC

Cuba lacks a strong tradition of manual folk crafts like weaving and pottery. What it does have, in amazing abundance and variety, is music that

Cuban musicians perform outside a building in Havana. As with many other aspects of the culture, Cuban music combines Spanish and African elements. Percussion instruments, such as the drums, bongos, bell, and *güiro* shown here, are a very important part of the music.

has become famous the world over. Like so many things Cuban, the music started as a mixture of African and Spanish elements. Slaves would use boxes to play the traditional rhythms of their African ancestors. Soon Spanish melodies and instruments like guitars joined the chorus—and the result was the rich music of Cuba.

Most Cuban music is built around the *clave*, a 1-2-3, 1-2 rhythm beaten out on wooden sticks. Lyrics often follow the forms of medieval Spanish poetry, with lines of 8 or 11 syllables.

The different types of music that developed include *son, danzón, mambo, cha-cha-cha,* and *rumba*. Percussion instruments such as conga or bongo drums, maracas, and the *güiro* (on which players scratch out the beat) are used in just about every type of music. Other instruments vary. The oldest songs, as well as the Cuban version of "country" music, use percussion, a standard guitar, and the *tres*, a special Cuban guitar with three sets of two strings. Other songs are played by *charanga* groups, which use percussion plus piano, bass, violins, and flute. Still other bands use a full-blown brass orchestra plus piano, bass, and, of course, percussion.

Cuba has also produced noteworthy novelists. Leading 20th-century writers include Guillermo Cabrera Infante, Heberto Padilla, Alejo Carpentier, and Dulce María Loinaz, winner of the Cervantes Prize, the most prestigious award for Spanish-language writers.

Cuba's notable modern painters include Wilfredo Lam, who studied with the world-famous Spanish artist Pablo Picasso, and Amalia Peláez.

TEXT-DEPENDENT QUESTIONS

1. What is the afternoon meal in Cuba called?
2. Why are so many 1950s-era American cars seen on the road in Cuba?

More than 11 million people live in Cuba, with most residing in cities and urban areas. (Opposite) A throng of enthusiastic Cubans wave flags as they parade through the streets of Havana during the annual Jose Martí political rally. (Right) A rural fishing village near Cienfuegos. This city on the southern coast of Cuba has a population of about 145,000.

5 CUBA'S CITIES

URBAN AREAS ARE home to three-fourths of Cuba's population, up from about 50 percent in the early 1950s. Just about all city dwellers have running water and electricity, but there are many blackouts—some scheduled, some unplanned—because of shortages of fuel and spare parts. Most residents of Cuba's cities work in government services, light industry, or tourism-related jobs.

HAVANA

With a population estimated at 2.1 million in 2015, Cuba's capital, Havana, is the largest of a dozen Cuban cities with more than 100,000 inhabitants. Havana was founded on Cuba's southern coast in 1515 by the Spanish explorer Diego Velázquez. It was moved to its present site on the northern coast four years later.

43

Havana became one of the most important cities in the Americas during the 16th and 17th centuries, when galleons laden with treasure from throughout the Spanish colonial empire gathered in its fine natural harbor before making the trip to Spain. The lighthouse fortress El Morro, the most recognized symbol of the city, dates from this era.

The city core, *Habana Vieja*, or Old Havana, is a maze of narrow streets and colonial architecture that includes the Cathedral of San Cristóbal de La Habana and the Palace of the Captains-General. Just on the other side of the still-visible 17th-century walls are the domed *Capitolio*, similar to the U.S. Capitol, and wide plazas with statues of patriots from Cuba's wars of independence. Beyond the central district are suburban neighborhoods like Marianao and Vedado. These feature broad boulevards such as the famous Malecón, a seaside drive that skirts Vedado from the old fortress of La Chorrera to another old fortress, La Punta, directly across from El Morro.

Among the city's attractions are the Colonial Art Museum, built in 1720 on Cathedral Square; the Museum of the Revolution, housed in the old Presidential Palace; and the Napoleonic Museum, which boasts one of the largest collections of Napoleonic-era *artifacts* outside of France.

Words to Understand in This Chapter

artifact—a man-made object of cultural or historical interest.
innovation—the process of making changes to something that has previously been established, such as by introducing new methods, ideas, or products.

American cars from the 1950s, such as these passing the capitol building in Havana, are commonly seen in Cuba. The Communist system makes it very expensive to buy a new car, and so Cubans have continued to drive vehicles that were on the road at the time of the Revolution.

SANTIAGO DE CUBA

Cuba's second-largest city, with a population of about 425,000, is on the eastern end of the island, near the Sierra Maestra. The mountain range's foothills give shape to Santiago itself, known for its steep streets with colonial architecture and magnificent views of the harbor. Among other Cubans, residents of Santiago are also known for their distinctive accent.

Founded in 1515, Santiago is today famed as a center of musical *innovation*. Musicians from Santiago created such renowned Cuban musical

DID YOU KNOW?

- The first known reference to tobacco by a European comes from the logbook of Christopher Columbus. In his entry for November 6, 1492, Columbus noted that two men he had sent to explore the interior of Cuba saw "many people who were going to different villages, men and women, carrying firebrands in their hands and herbs to smoke, which they are in a habit of doing."
- In honor of one of his royal patrons, King Fernando of Spain, Columbus gave the island of Cuba the name Fernandina. Later explorers referred to the island as Juana, a popular woman's name in Spanish. Eventually the Spanish adopted the name Cuba, which they believed was what the Indians called the island.

styles as the *son*, the *conga*, and the *trova*.

A house reputed to be Cuba's oldest structure, the early-16th-century home of conquistador Diego Velázquez, today hosts the Museum of Historical Cuban Ambiance, featuring colonial furniture and decorative objects. Also in Santiago is Antonio Maceo's Birthplace, a museum displaying artifacts from the life of the 19th-century hero of independence; and the Emilio Bacardí Provincial Museum, which boasts a collection of Cuban paintings. Near the city is the much-visited sanctuary to La Virgen de la Caridad (the Virgin of Charity), Cuba's patron saint.

CAMAGÜEY

Mention Camagüey to Cubans, and they immediately think of *tinajones*. The city is famous for its pot-bellied barrels made of oven-fired clay, which in past centuries stored water. As many as 16,000 *tinajones* stood in front yards

The city hall in Santiago de Cuba, the island's second-largest city.

throughout the city in 1900. About 2,000 remain, now displayed as decorations and symbols of local pride. Locals also take pride in living in the hometown of Ignacio Agramonte, a hero of the Ten Years War; his birthplace is now a museum. Camagüey was founded in 1814 in a region of cattle ranches. It is Cuba's third-largest city, with an estimated 306,000 residents in 2015.

BAYAMO

Although its estimated 147,500 residents make it only Cuba's eighth-largest city, Bayamo has a prominent place in Cuban history. It was in a sugar mill outside of town called Demajagua that the Ten Years War began. In 1868, Cuban independence fighters burned down Bayamo rather than turn it over to enemy troops. Also nearby at Dos Ríos, a monument marks the site where national

Cathedral San Isidoro is located in Peralta Park, Holguín.

hero José Martí was killed in battle in 1895. Going back further in time, Bayamo holds the distinction of being Cuba's second-oldest city, with only the small town of Baracoa—founded on the northeastern coast by conquistador Diego Velázquez—being older.

OTHER CITIES

Other important eastern cities include **Holguín** (with a 2015 population of about 277,000) and **Guantánamo** (population: 208,000), which is located outside the U.S. naval base. Situated by the Escambray Mountains, **Santa Clara**, with about 205,000 residents, is the largest city in central Cuba.

In the west, **Pinar del Río**, a city of 137,000, has become a center for nature-loving tourists who want to explore nearby reserves and the spectacular Viñales Valley. Those more interested in simply kicking back gravitate toward **Varadero**, Cuba's most famous beach. Varadero is located on a narrow peninsula on the northern coast, between **Cárdenas**, a city of about 81,000 known as the place where the Cuban flag was first raised on Cuban soil, and **Matanzas**, a seaport and provincial capital inhabited by some 133,000 residents, which was founded in 1693.

The colonial town of Trinidad is a popular tourist destination.

Among smaller towns, **Trinidad** is noteworthy. Its colonial streets and buildings, practically intact since the 1700s, make the entire city a magnificent outdoor museum. Trinidad also boasts at least four "indoor" museums celebrating the city's heritage.

TEXT-DEPENDENT QUESTIONS

1. What Spanish explorer founded Havana? In what year was the city established?
2. What is Cuba's third-largest city? What is this city known for among Cubans?
3. What national hero was killed at Bayamo in 1895?

Throughout the Spanish-speaking world, small cities and large towns alike have for centuries held colorful annual fiestas to honor their patron saint. In Cuba this practice came to an end in the 1960s, when the Cuban Revolution took power and ended religious festivities.

Old festivals have been replaced by holidays honoring heroes of the Revolution and by cultural festivals that are not necessarily held annually. In addition, commemorations of patriots and historic events from the 19th-century struggles for independence have been important celebrations ever since Cuba became a republic in 1902.

JANUARY

New Year's Day is also celebrated throughout Cuba as the anniversary of the **Triumph of the Revolution**, the day in 1959 when Fidel Castro took power.

Traditionally, parents gave their children gifts on January 6, which was celebrated as **Three Kings Day**, but under Castro that tradition has died out.

January 28 marks the **Birthday of José Martí**, Cuba's national hero. Schoolchildren honor Martí's memory by reciting his poems in special assemblies.

FEBRUARY

During **Carnival**, a celebration that takes place before the Catholic Lenten season (which may begin in February or March), Cuban cities hold parades with conga dancers and colorful floats. The most famous celebrations are those held in Havana and Santiago.

February 24 is the anniversary of the start of the **War of Independence.**

MARCH

Cubans observe March 13 as **Ataque a Palacio**, the day in 1957 when a group of students attacked dictator Fulgencio Batista in Havana's Presidential Palace.

Catholicism's **Holy Week** can take place in March or April, but traditional processions are rare now. Cuban Catholics pass **Good Friday** and **Easter Sunday** quietly in church.

APRIL

Bay of Pigs Day, April 19, celebrates the defeat of U.S.-sponsored anti-Castro invaders in 1961.

MAY

The first of May is **May Day**, the International Worker's Day. The Cuban government organizes large parades.

On May 3 and 4, people in Holguín hold **Romerías de Mayo**. This celebration of the town's Spanish heritage features food and music and takes place on a hill called Loma de la Cruz. Yet another traditional celebration is **Fiesta de las Flores**, the Feast of the Flowers, in Santa Clara.

May 20 is **Independence Day**. Although it is no longer an official holiday, some Cubans still celebrate it.

JUNE

Since 1856 Camagüey has held its **Agricultural Fair** in June at the Casino Campestre. Residents also observe **San Juan Camagüeyano** between the 24th and 29th of the month with a public fiesta featuring a ceramics exhibit and the eating of a traditional vegetable-and-meat stew called *ajiaco*. Some small towns hold their carnivals around this same week, instead of before Lent.

JULY

July 26 marks the anniversary of Castro's unsuccessful attack on Batista's army barracks in Moncada. Called the **Start of the Revolution**, it is the most important official holiday and features marches and long speeches from leaders.

AUGUST

Verbena de la Calle Gloria, held in the city of Santa Clara on August 16, is one of the oldest local public fiestas still celebrated.

OCTOBER

October's special occasions include solemn ceremonies for two revolutionary leaders on the anniversaries of their deaths. On October 8, Cubans honor **Ernesto "Che" Guevara**, the Argentine physician and aide to Castro, who died in 1967 while attempting to foment a revolution in Bolivia. On October 28, 1959, an airplane carrying **Camilo Cienfuegos**, one of Castro's key commanders, disappeared over the ocean during a flight from Camagüey to Havana. Each year on the 28th, Cuban children throw flowers into the sea, saying, "Una flor por Camilo" ("A flower for Camilo").

October 10 is the anniversary of the start of the **Ten Years War**.

NOVEMBER

During the second week in November, Santa Clara holds **Semana de la Cultura** (Culture Week), with exhibitions of local crafts.

A day of national mourning is held on November 27 to commemorate the **Execution of Eight Medical Students** by the Spanish colonial government.

DECEMBER

Another day of mourning occurs on December 7, which marks the **Death of Antonio Maceo** during the War of Independence.

In Remedios, the mid-December tradition of **Parrandas** survives. During this time, groups of neighbors gather to sing and visit nearby neighborhoods.

Christmas began to be observed again in 1998, more than 30 years after the government banned celebrations. But food shortages make it difficult to serve the traditional Christmas Eve meal of rice and beans and roast pork.

Black Bean Soup

1 lb dried black beans
2 bay leaves
1 green bell pepper, chopped
4 cloves of garlic, minced
1 onion, chopped
1 tsp cumin
1 tsp vinegar
1 tsp sugar (optional)
1/2 cup olive oil
Salt and ground pepper to taste
1 quart water

Directions:

1. Soak beans overnight in the water.
2. The next day, drain and rinse the beans with fresh water. Fill the pot with enough water to cover the beans by 1 1/2 to 2 inches.
3. Put in bay leaves and boil until tender, about 2 hours. Lower heat to a simmer.
4. Sauté the bell pepper, garlic, and onion until soft. Add cumin and stir, cooking a few moments more. Add this mix, called the *sofrito*, to the simmering beans.
5. Stir in vinegar and sugar, and season with salt and pepper.
6. Cook over low heat for about 45 minutes more.
7. Serve as soup or over rice.

Cuban Steak

4 steaks (a Cuban butcher cut called *palomilla* is best, but thinly cut top round will also work)
2 cloves garlic, minced
Salt and pepper to taste
Juice of 2 limes
1/2 cup olive oil
4 tsp chopped fresh parsley

Directions:

1. Pound the steaks with a mallet until they are about 1/2 inch thick. Season with garlic, salt, and pepper and marinate in lime juice overnight in the refrigerator.
2. In a large frying pan, heat the oil until sizzling. Sauté the steaks over medium heat until browned.
3. When ready to serve, sprinkle fresh parsley on top.

Medianoche (Midnight Sandwich)

Ham
Swiss cheese
Roast pork or cooked pork loin
Soft egg buns
Mustard
Mayonnaise
Butter

Directions:

1. Spread mustard on one side of an egg bun and mayonnaise on the other.
2. Place two slices each of ham, Swiss cheese, and

roast pork or cooked pork loin on the bun.

3. Spread a little butter on top of the crust.

4. Place the bun on a baking sheet and flatten with a skillet, heavy pan, or spatula.

5. Bake in an oven at 350°F until the cheese is melted and the bread crispy and hot.

Tostones (Cuban Fried Plantains)

Plantains (available in Hispanic food stores and, increasingly, in supermarkets)
Cooking oil
Salt

Directions:

1. Peel an unripe green plantain and slice it into round pieces about 1/2 inch wide.

2. Fry in hot oil until color begins to turn gold.

3. Take out of oil, cover with wax paper or a brown paper bag, and pound flat, about 1/2 inch thick, with a kitchen mallet or a heavy can.

4. Add salt to taste, return to hot oil, and cook until golden and soft.

You can also cook ripe plantains the same way, resulting in a dish that is mushy and sweet called *plátanos maduros fritos*.

Cuban Roast Pork

One leg of pork (5–6 pounds)
1/2 cup fresh lime juice
1/2 cup fresh orange juice
4–6 cloves of garlic
1 tbsp salt
1 tsp cumin
1 tsp oregano

Directions:

1. Pour the juices over the leg of pork.

2. Mash together the garlic, salt, cumin, and oregano until they form a thick paste. Rub the paste into the meat.

3. Marinate pork overnight in refrigerator.

4. Roast at 350°F for one hour, then turn down to 325° and insert a meat thermometer. Cook for an additional three hours or until the internal temperature reaches 180°. Add wine if the meat starts getting dry.

Amerindian—a term for the indigenous peoples of North, Central, and South America, including the Caribbean islands, before the arrival of Europeans in the late 15th century.

cay—a low island or reef made from sand or coral.

civil liberty—the right of people to do or say things that are not illegal without being stopped or interrupted by the government.

conquistador—any one of the Spanish leaders of the conquest of the Americas in the 1500s.

Communism—a political system in which all resources, industries, and property are considered to be held in common by all the people, with government as the central authority responsible for controlling all economic and social activity.

coup d'état—the violent overthrow of an existing government by a small group.

deforestation—the action or process of clearing forests.

economic system—the production, distribution, and consumption of goods and services within a country.

ecotourism—a form of tourism in which resorts attempt to minimize the impact of visitors on the local environment, contribute to conserving habitats, and employ local people.

embargo—a government restriction or restraint on commerce, especially an order that prohibits trade with a particular nation.

exploit—to take advantage of something; to use something unfairly.

foreign aid—financial assistance given by one country to another.

free trade—trade based on the unrestricted exchange of goods, with tariffs (taxes) only used to create revenue, not keep out foreign goods.

hurricane—a very powerful and destructive storm, characterized by high winds and significant rainfall, that often occurs in the western Atlantic Ocean and the Caribbean Sea between June and November.

leeward—a side that is sheltered or away from the wind.

mestizo—a person of mixed Amerindian and European (typically Spanish) descent.

offshore banking—a term applied to banking transactions conducted between participants located outside of a country. Such transactions Some Caribbean countries have become known for this practice thanks to their banking laws.

plaza—the central open square at the center of colonial-era cities in Latin America.

plebiscite—a vote by which the people of an entire country express their opinion on a particular government or national policy.

population density—a measurement of the number of people living in a specific area, such a square mile or square kilometer.

pre-Columbian—referring to a time before the 1490s, when Christopher Columbus landed in the Americas.

regime—a period of rule by a particular government, especially one that is considered to be oppressive.

service industry—any business, organization, or profession that does work for a customer, but is not involved in manufacturing.

windward—the side or direction from which the wind is blowing.

Cuban Culture Box

Draw the flag of Cuba on a piece of paper and paste it on the lid of a cigar box or a shoebox. Glue pictures of Cuba on the sides. Find 4 to 6 items that reflect the culture of Cuba and put them inside—these can include a CD of Cuban music, a book by a Cuban author, or postcards of Havana. Write half a page explaining what each item is. Staple the pages together into a booklet with a cover and put it inside the box too.

Cuban Patriots Report

Find pictures of the patriots listed below (all of whom played a role in Cuba's wars of independence), and write a three- or four-paragraph biography of each:

- José Martí
- Máximo Gómez
- Antonio Maceo
- Calixto García
- Carlos Manuel de Céspedes
- Tomás Estrada Palma

Politics Report

Research the history of Castro's revolution. Make a list of the good things it has done for Cuba. Make a list of the bad things. Which are more important? Why? Write a five- to six-paragraph report. If there are Cubans living in your area, you can interview them. Or you can write to some of the groups listed in the "For More Information" section to get their opinions.

Cuban Birds

Find pictures of six bird species endemic to Cuba. Write one paragraph on each, and glue the appropriate picture next to each paragraph.

Cuban Geography Map

Draw a map of Cuba on cardboard or poster board. Stick on dot labels to show the locations of the 10 largest cities, using labels of different colors to indicate size. With papier-mâché, build up the mountain areas and color them dark green. Color the savannas light green.

Cuban Music

Find examples of the following types of Cuban music:

- Son
- Guajira
- Bolero
- Cha-cha-chá
- Zapateo
- Danzón
- Mambo
- Rumba

Play selections of the music for the class and present a report explaining how each style is different. See if you can tell which instruments are used. The music link under "Internet Resources" is a good start.

Cuban Habitat Map

Draw a large map of Cuba. Use different colors to mark four kinds of habitat: swamp, mountain, seashore, and savanna. For each habitat, write in the names of at least four animals that live there. If possible, include one mammal, one reptile, one bird, and one mollusk.

1492	Christopher Columbus lands on the island of Cuba on October 27.
1510s	Diego Velázquez begins the Spanish conquest and colonization of Cuba; he establishes a handful of towns, including Baracoa and Santiago, and serves as the colony's governor.
1519	Havana is founded in its present location after being moved there from the southern coast.
mid-1500s	Indian mortality is nearly 100 percent; African slaves are brought to replace Indian workers.
1762	British troops take Havana, returning it to Spain the following year.
early 1800s	First Cuban independence conspiracies are crushed.
1850	Narciso López, a Venezuelan-born general, mounts an unsuccessful expedition to free Cuba from Spanish rule.
1868–78	Ten Years War; Cuban rebels defeated.
1880s	Colonial government ignores promised reform; José Martí, Cuba's national hero, begins organizing new independence struggle in the United States.
1886	Slavery in Cuba is abolished.
1895	War of Independence starts; Martí is killed in battle.
1898	After the sinking of the battleship *Maine* in Havana Harbor, the United States declares war on Spain and, along with Cuban independence fighters, defeats Spanish forces in Cuba. American occupation of Cuba begins.
1902	American occupation ends; Cuba is declared independent.
1902–06	Presidency of Tomás Estrada Palma.
1906–09	Second U.S. intervention.
1909–30	Conservative and Liberal parties govern relatively stable nation.
1930–33	Machado dictatorship.
1934	The Platt Amendment, which allows U.S. intervention in Cuban affairs, is abolished by American president Franklin D. Roosevelt.
1933–40	Fulgencio Batista wields power as behind-the-scenes strongman.
1940–52	New constitution; period of democratic but corrupt rule; economy flourishes.
1952–58	Batista dictatorship.

1959	Fidel Castro takes power.
1960	Private property nationalized, press censored; political jailings and executions.
1961	A U.S.-sponsored army of Cuban exiles is defeated at the Bay of Pigs.
1962	United States imposes economic embargo; Cuban Missile Crisis.
1965	Beginning of "Freedom Flights" that will bring 250,000 exiles to the United States over the next eight years.
1960s–80s	Cuba sponsors guerrilla movements in Latin America; Cuban troops fight with Communist rebels in Africa.
1980	Mariel boatlift brings 125,000 Cubans to the United States.
1991	Fall of Soviet communism deprives Cuba of political and economic support.
1992	With Cuba's economy in a tailspin, Castro permits some market-oriented reform.
1994	Rafter Crisis: 32,000 Cubans escape to Florida in homemade rafts.
1996	Members of dissident Concilio Cubano movement are jailed; Cuban Air Force shoots down two civilian aircraft piloted by Cuban-Americans; United States toughens embargo.
1998	Pope John Paul II visits Havana.
2000	Seven-year-old Elián González is returned to Cuba after a bitter political battle in Miami.
2002	Former president Jimmy Carter visits Cuba, expressing his hopes for better U.S.-Cuba relations but calling for political reforms by the Castro government.
2005	A U.S. appellate court overturns the 2001 convictions of five Cubans accused of espionage activities in the United States.
2008	Fidel Castro retires; his brother, Raúl, takes his place as president.
2010	Dissidents stage hunger strikes in an attempt to force the release of political prisoners.
2012	Pope Benedict XVI visits Cuba, and calls for greater freedom on the island.
2014	Russian President Vladimir Putin visits Cuba, and says that Moscow will cancel billions of dollars of Cuban debt dating from the Soviet era.
2015	The U.S. government eases some travel and trade restrictions related to Cuba, and diplomats from the two countries meet for discussions about restoring relations. In September Pope Francis visits Cuba.

Bondil, Nathalie. *Cuba: Art and History from 1868 to Today*. New York: Prestel, 2008.

Cooke, Julia. *The Other Side of Paradise: Life in the New Cuba*. Berkeley, Calif.: Seal Press, 2014.

Heuman, Gad. *The Caribbean: A Brief History*. New York: Bloomsbury, 2014.

Keen, Benjamin, and Keith Haynes. *A History of Latin America.* Boston: Wadsworth Cengage Learning, 2013.

Sainsbury, Brendan. *Cuba*. Oakland, Calif.: Lonely Planet, 2015.

Sublette, Ned. *Cuba and Its Music: From the First Drums to the Mambo*. Chicago: Chicago Review Press, 2007.

History and Geography

http://lcweb.loc.gov/rr/hispanic/1898/
http://www.historyofcuba.com/cuba.htm

Economic and Political Information

http://www.usacubatravel.com/cuba.htm
http://www.state.gov/r/pa/ei/bgn/2886.htm
https://www.cia.gov/library/publications/the-world-factbook/geos/cu.html

Culture and Festivals

http://icuban.com/index.html
http://www.mamborama.com/cuba_music.html
http://www.herenciaculturalcubana.org/HTML_pages/English/Main.html

**Cuban Interests Section
in the United States**
2630 16th Street, NW
Washington, DC 20009
Tel: 202-797-8518
Fax: 202-797-8521
Email: recepcion@sicuw.org
Website: www.cubadiplomatica.cu

Cuba Tourist Board in Canada
1200 Bay Street. Suite 305.
Toronto, ON M5R 2A5
Canada
Tel: 416-362-0700
Fax: 416-362-6799
Email: info@gocuba.ca
Website: www.gocuba.ca

Cuban-American National Council
1223 SW Fourth Street
Miami, FL 33135
Tel: 305-642-3484
Fax: 305-642-9122
Email: slopez@cnc.org
Website: www.cnc.org

Senior Consulting Editor **James D. Henderson** is professor of international studies at Coastal Carolina University. He is the author of *Conservative Thought in Twentieth Century Latin America: The Ideals of Laureano Gómez* (1988; Spanish edition *Las ideas de Laureano Gómez* published in 1985); *When Colombia Bled: A History of the Violence in Tolima* (1985; Spanish edition *Cuando Colombia se desangró, una historia de la Violencia en metrópoli y provincia*, 1984); and coauthor of *A Reference Guide to Latin American History* (2000) and *Ten Notable Women of Latin America* (1978).

Mr. Henderson earned a bachelor's degree in history from Centenary College of Louisiana, and a master's degree in history from the University of Arizona. He then spent three years in the Peace Corps, serving in Colombia, before earning his doctorate in Latin American history in 1972 at Texas Christian University.

Roger E. Hernández writes a nationally syndicated column distributed by King Features to newspapers across the country and is coauthor of *Cubans in America*, an illustrated history of the Cuban presence in the United States. He also teaches writing and journalism at the New Jersey Institute of Technology and Rutgers University.